Man

This book belongs to

_____

Written by Stephen Barnett
Illustrated by Rosie Brooks

Pegasus
An imprint of
B. Jain Publishers (P) Ltd.
An ISO 9001:2000 Certified Company

Contents

About this Book

This book helps children learn about good manners apart from enhancing their language skills and vocabulary. Colourful illustrations add to the beauty of this book and helps in the better understanding of the learners.

Manners

Please

Thank you

It is good manners to say please and thank you.

Please may I have the book?

Thank you for the apple.

Can I help you?

Thank you for your help.

You are welcome.

Let me open the door for you.

Thank you for opening the door.

Please may I have some cake?

Thank you for the cake.

Two little magical words...

...please and thank you.

New Words

apple	open
cake	please
door	thank you
have	welcome
magical	words
manners	

What did you learn?

What is the colour of the book?

What does the boy open?

What is the colour of the cake?

What are the two magical words?